9.99

BIG JETS

Osprey Colour Series

B-2448

BIG JETS

Norman Pealing

Published in 1987 by Osprey Publishing Limited
59 Grosvenor Street, London W1X 9DA
Reprinted spring 1989 and summer 1990

British Library Cataloguing in Publication Data

Pealing, Norman
  Big jets. — (Osprey colour series)
  1. Transport planes
  I. Title
  629.133'340423   TL685.4

ISBN 0-85045-725-4

Editor Dennis Baldry
Designed by David Tarbutt
Printed in Hong Kong

Front cover Gear down, slattery and flappery
extended, a TWA 747 'Skyliner' prepares for
touchdown

Title pages Kai Tak, Hong Kong: no
mistaking the Pan Am 747 amid the bustle of
this famous international airport

Back cover Jumbo sunset (747-300)

Right A WW2-vintage North American B-25
Mitchell bomber enabled the author to
photograph a Northwest Airlines' Boeing
757 air-to-air during the preparation of *BIG
JETS*. One of the Mitchell's two 1700 hp
Wright R-2600 Double Cyclone 14-cylinder
two-row radials rumbles in the foreground as
the 757 holds station behind

For a catalogue of all books published by Osprey Aerospace
please write to:

**The Marketing Manager, Consumer Catalogue Department
Osprey Publishing Ltd, 59 Grosvenor Street, London, W1X 9DA**

Norman Pealing FRPS began taking pictures 'too long ago', but his interest in aviation was not kindled until he joined the Royal Air Force in 1958. In those days, V-bombers and photography didn't mix unless you wanted a spell behind bars, in which case you ended up without a single photograph anyway.

In 1965 Norman Pealing joined the British Aircraft Corporation (BAC) and began making sales/publicity films to promote all the company's products, which included guided weapons, satellites, military and civil aircraft. He attended many first flights and took part in the demonstration tours of the One-Eleven and Concorde airliners. In 1983 he chose to leave what had become the Weybridge Division of British Aerospace (BAe) to form his own company at Fairoaks Airport in Surrey. Norman Pealing Limited specializes in aviation photography and film/video production for advertising, sales, public relations, publishing, and television requirements.

The photographs in *BIG JETS* were all taken with Hasselblad cameras and lenses, loaded with Ektachrome EPN 100 roll film.

Right The world's only all Rolls-Royce RB.211-powered airline, Cathay Pacific is justly renowned for its technical excellence and superb service. Based in Hong Kong, the carrier has operated the 747-200B since July 1979. All Cathay's 747s are powered by the RB.211-524D4 version

Contents

747: first and foremost

Boeing sold their 747th 747 jetliner in the summer of 1986 and production continues at the rate of three per month. The 747 is unquestionably one of the all-time greats in the history of aviation. When the first 747 entered service in January 1970 it changed the shape of air travel and opened new horizons for millions of people around the world. Today the 747 is more than just an airliner — it is an icon of Western culture and a flying advertisement for The American

Way. With the advent of the 747-400 and yet more derivations, a production run exceeding 1000 units is no pipedream. **These pages** A 747B Combi of the Civil Aviation Administration of China (CAAC) approaches Hong Kong International Airport

9

CAAC operate regular services to more than 20 countries, including Hong Kong. Sovereignty of the British Colony will revert to China in 1997 and CAAC is expected to assume a more dominant role after the handover

Right A captain's eye view on the flight deck of a British Airways' 747-200

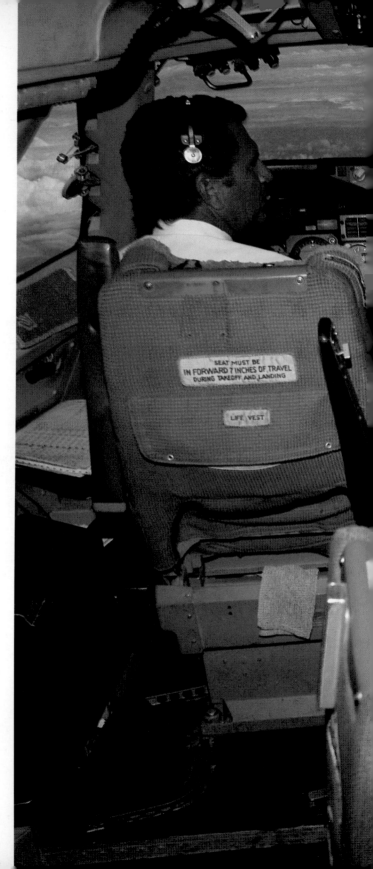

The flight deck of a Singapore Airlines'
747-300 'Big Top', replete with familiar
anolog instrumentation; the flight engineer
(now a vanishing breed) has volume 1B of
the Boeing 747 Operations Manual at the
ready in the unlikely event of any serious
technical problems. A digital flight deck or
'glass cockpit' featuring CRT displays will be
standard equipment on the 747-400

Left The flight engineer's panel on the 747-300: it may look intimidating at first glance, but it enables the operator to monitor the aircraft's vital signs and 'fine tune' the engines for optimum efficiency

A passenger's eye view from the same aircraft

Flanked by an Airbus, the Big Top disgorges its passengers at Singapore Changi Airport

Right Hauled into a 37-degree right-hand turn, a Singapore Airlines' 747-200 makes a classic 'fighter approach' into Hong Kong. The runway is surrounded on three sides by water and an accurate approach is vital. Few passengers forget this intimate encounter with the Hong Kong skyline

Left Northwest 747 prior to push-back at the airline's Minneapolis St Paul base

Singapore Airlines' 747-200 taxies at Hong Kong against the backdrop of the harbour and a wall of skyscrapers; a container ship rides at anchor

Northwest trio: a 747 (foreground) shares the ramp with a DC-10 at Minneapolis St Paul as a 727 climbs out in the distance

These pages and overleaf A UTA 747 arriving at Paris Charles De Gaulle Airport. The aircraft in the foreground (left) are BAC One-Eleven 500s operated by British Airways; the nearest example has hushkits for its Spey turbofans. UTA is the largest independent airline in France and it operates scheduled passenger and freight services to Africa, the Middle East, Far East, and the American west coast

Preceding pages Night shift: a Flying Tigers' 747F swallows a cargo pallet at Boston. **This page** On finals for Hong Kong after a long haul. The all-cargo carrier was formed in 1945 by an ex-member of the American Volunteer Group's 'Flying Tigers' which fought against the Japanese in China. **Right** SAA 747s parked at London Heathrow Airport in company with a Concorde (background)

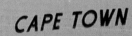

Right and opposite page South African Airways operate a mixed fleet of 747s. For the 747-300 (right) SAA chose Pratt & Whitney JT9D-7R4G2 turbofans, each rated at 54,750 lb (244 kN) of thrust

Below A TWA 747 'Skyliner' stabilized on the approach with its main gear extended like some giant four-legged bird of prey. This particular aircraft is also featured on the front cover

Preceding pages Sydney, Australia (left): Qantas selected Rolls-Royce RB.211-524D4s for its 747-300s. London Heathrow (right): a Jumbo shadow courtesy of Seaboard World and (inset) an Air India 747 prepares to take off from Runway 28R

These pages Two contrasting views of a Pan
Am 747 descending into Hong Kong

Pan Am has a fleet of 48 747s, including 11 of the ultra long-range 747SP (special performance) version pictured here wearing the airline's older, more understated titles at Hong Kong. A US Navy Lockheed P-3C Orion anti-submarine patrol aircraft is visible in the background (below)

Japan Air Lines (left) and All Nippon Airways (opposite page) are respectively the world's largest 747 operator and the largest airline in Japan. **Below** Photographed from the flight deck of a 747, an Alitalia 747 Combi takes on freight at Chicago O'Hare

Left Walking the Jumbo? Groundcrew prepare to pull the chocks from the nose gear of British Airways' 747 *City of Bristol*

United 747SP nuzzles the gate at Melbourne, Australia

Northwest 747 at Boston: the carrier kicked off some $7 billion worth of orders for 60 747-400s when it ordered the first 10 examples in October 1985. The other customers include SIA, KLM, Lufthansa, and British Airways

Right A mixed bag at Boston, consisting of a Zantop L-188 Electra turboprop, a TWA L-1011, a Swissair 747-300, and a Lufthansa 747-200. Surviving Electras are mainly used as cargo aircraft, but the type was originally designed by one Clarence L 'Kelly' Johnson of SR-71 Blackbird fame as a short- to medium-range airliner, the prototype of which first flew in February 1958. The Electra is survived by the derived P-3 Orion maritime reconnaissance aircraft, which will probably stay in production until the end of the century

Qantas' *City of Dubbo* is pushed back at Melbourne as an Alitalia Jumbo looks on

Right A Thai Airways International 747 turns in towards the gate at Melbourne in between showers

Boeing twins

The 757 made its maiden flight in February 1982 and entered service in December 1982. Sales passed the 200-mark in 1987. Delta placed a record $3 billion order for 60 757s in 1980 and one of their immaculate fleet is pictured at Memphis, Tennessee

The 757 is arguably the most elegant airliner
Boeing have produced since the classic 707.
A Northwest example displays its sleek lines
over Tucson, Arizona (left), and arriving at a
wintry Minneapolis St Paul

Northwest specified Pratt & Whitney
PW2037 engines (each rated at 38,200 lb
[170 kN] of thrust) to power its 757s. The
757 can accommodate up to 239 passengers
and has a wing span of 125 ft 10 in (38.05 m)
and a length of 159 ft 2 in (47.32 m). At
takeoff, the 757 tips the scales at 240,000 lb
(108,800 kg)

50

This page Snow problem for Northwest's *Cities of Tampa Bay*. **Overleaf, left** People get confused. One diffident passenger had to be reassured by an ever-friendly Northwest flight attendant: 'No madam, this plane isn't going to New York' ... **Overleaf, right** This British Airways' 757 appears to be crabbing slightly into wind as it nears the approach lights in the foreground. Gear still up, the 747 trailing behind will be the next to land. Some 38 big jets arrive at London Heathrow Airport during the peak two-hour period every morning

Singapore Airlines' fleet of four PW 2037-powered 757s fly to Medan, Jakarta, Kuantan, Penang, and Kuala Lumpur. These pictures were taken at the latter location

The 767 flew some five months before the 757, on 26 September 1981. ER (extended range) versions seem to be catching on, taking sales of all 767 models over the 200-mark in 1986. Customers for the 767-200ER include Chinese flag carrier CAAC and the aircraft is available with Pratt & Whitney JT9D-7R4E or General Electric CF6-80A2 turbofans, both rated at 50,000 lb (222 kN) of thrust

Qantas flies the 767-200ER non-stop between Perth and Tokyo. This is *City of Lake Macquarie*

Right 'The world's only *six-star* airline', Ansett Airlines of Australia became a wide-bodied outfit when their first 767-200 arrived in 1986. The design of the attractive motif on the tail was inspired by the Australian national flag

Qantas selected the Pratt & Whitney JT9D-7R4E for its 767-200ERs

Right The flight deck of the 767-200ER, complete with CRT displays. This Qantas example is over Sydney Harbour

Qantas' 767-200ER approaching the main runway at Sydney's Kingsford Smith Airport

Air Pacific 747 landing at Melbourne,
watched by the captain of a Qantas' 767

Airbus: the European challenge

Some said it would never be built. Some said it would never fly. Some said it would never be certificated. Some said it would never sell. They were wrong. The A300 was built, it did fly (28 October 1972), it was certificated (March 1974), and today over 370 Airbuses are flying the line. Combined orders for the A300/A310 stand at over 520

The A320 made its maiden flight one month ahead of schedule in February 1987 with a backlog of commitments exceeding 460 aircraft. **Left** The A300 helped Iberia back from the brink. **Above** Air Afrique A300 arriving at Paris Charles De Gaulle Airport

A Cyprus Airways' A310 is refuelled and loaded with freight containers at the carrier's Larnaca base. The aircraft is powered by a pair of General Electric CF6-80C2-A2 turbofans, each rated at 53,500 lb (237 kN) of thrust. Pratt & Whitney engines are also available

Right A general view of the turnround operation illustrated on the preceding pages, with a KLM A310 in the background. **Inset** The aircraft climbs out, bound for London. The main gears are just starting to retract. **Below** The cockpit of the A310 is second to none. The lower CRT screen includes speed, attitude, and height (flight level) information; the upper screen displays waypoints and ground track for navigation

An A310-300 operated by Balair (Swissair's charter subsidiary) parked outside the main terminal at Basel-Mulhouse Airport in the summer of 1986

Left The A310-300's wingtip fences make the aerofoil even more efficient by minimizing induced drag. **Bottom left** The A310 retains the basic eight-abreast twin aisle fuselage cross-section of the A300 series. **Below** The powerplants are Pratt & Whitney JT9D-7R4E1 turbofans each developing 50,000 lb (223 kN) of thrust. **Right** The A310-300 is the first production airliner with a tailplane trim tank (less drag) and a carbonfibre fin (less weight). The A310-300 can carry 218 passengers 4500 nm (8350 km), a 500 nm (930 km) improvement over the A300-200

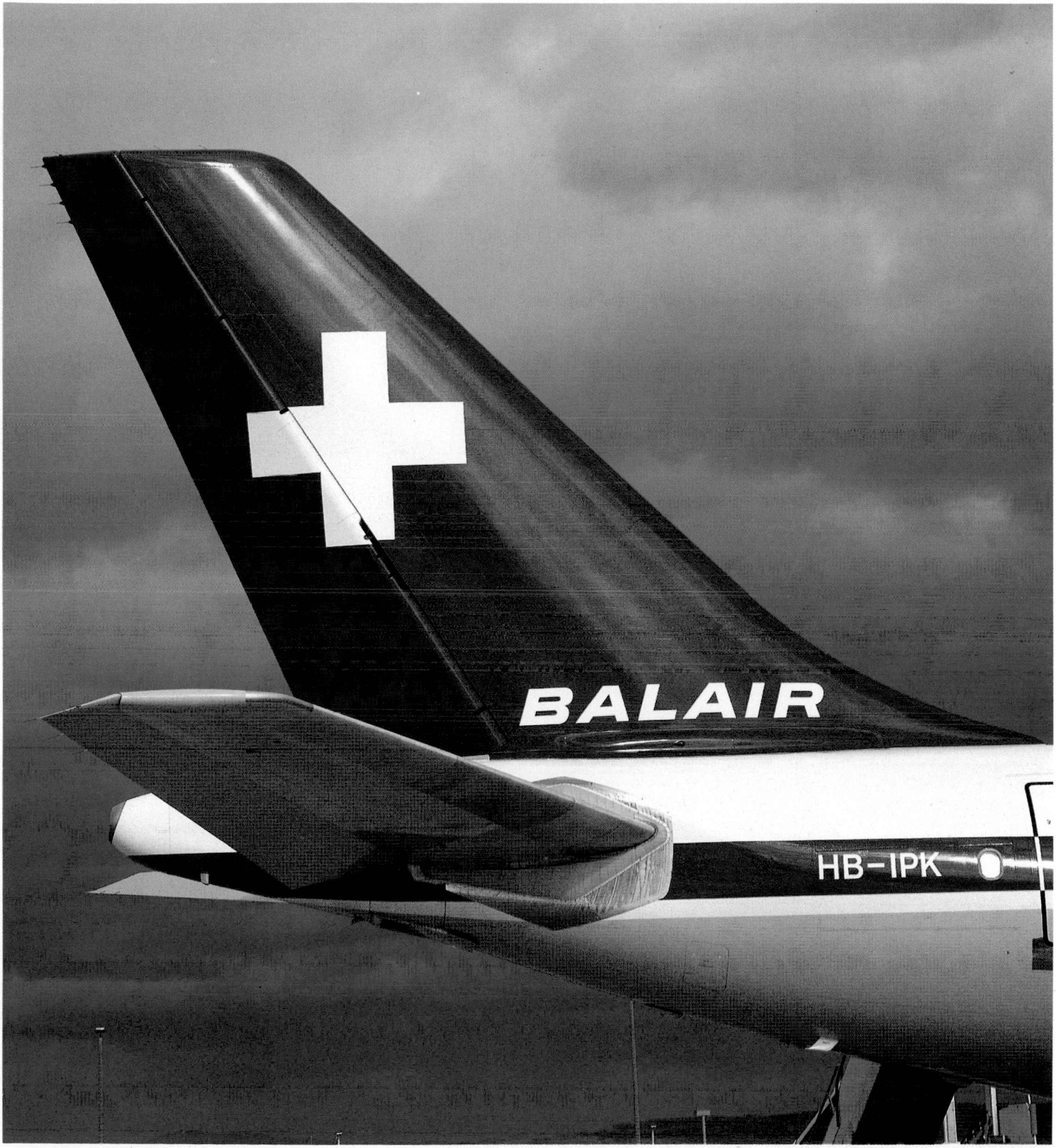
BALAIR
HB-IPK

A Thai Airways International A300 awaits
its passengers at Hong Kong before departing
on the 2 hour 30 minute flight to Bangkok
(right)

Preceding pages and right Thai A300s bask outside the carrier's maintenance hangars at Bangkok

These pages A Malaysian Airline System A300 burns rubber as it brings in 300 tourists to Penang, the island resort off the coast of Malaya

Overleaf The embryonic Emirates Airlines utilize an A300 to operate a scheduled service between Dubai and Pakistan

83

Indian Airlines have a fleet of 10 A300s and the carrier has 19 A320s on order. The airline was formed in 1953, having taken over the domestic and regional services previously operated by eight private airlines. Not surprisingly, it enjoys an extensive route network within the Indian subcontinent in addition to its operations to the Maldive Islands, Sri Lanka, Bangladesh, Pakistan, Nepal and Afghanistan. This A300 is taxying out at Calcutta in front of a Fokker F.27 Friendship parked in the background

Left Like the majority of A300s, Indian Airlines' fleet are fitted with General Electric CF6-50C2 turbofans rated at 52,500 lb (233 kN) of thrust

Another Indian Airlines' A300, this time captured during a floodlit turnround at Delhi

Left and above A Kuwait Airways' A300 unloads passengers and cargo at Kuwait International Airport. The Middle East carrier is one of a small number of airlines which operate a mixed fleet of A300s and Boeing 767s

Overleaf The attractive livery of the Civil Aviation Administration of China is displayed to advantage by this A310 at Hong Kong

The same CAAC A310 depicted on the previous page on finals over Kowloon, Hong Kong

Overleaf Korean Air began operating the A300 in 1975. This example stands ready before another departure from Hong Kong to serve the carrier's Far East network

94

Taiwan-based China Airlines operate regular services to Hong Kong with A300s

Right The whale-like elegance of the Airbus is exemplified by this Alitalia A300 (which carries the appropriate registration I-BUSG) as it climbs away from Heathrow

The big trijets

Left The awesome sight of a Northwest DC-10, photographed in the vicinity of Rochester, Minnesota, from the open door of a Piper Aztec

One of Northwest's 19 DC-10s parked at a distinctly chilly Minneapolis St Paul

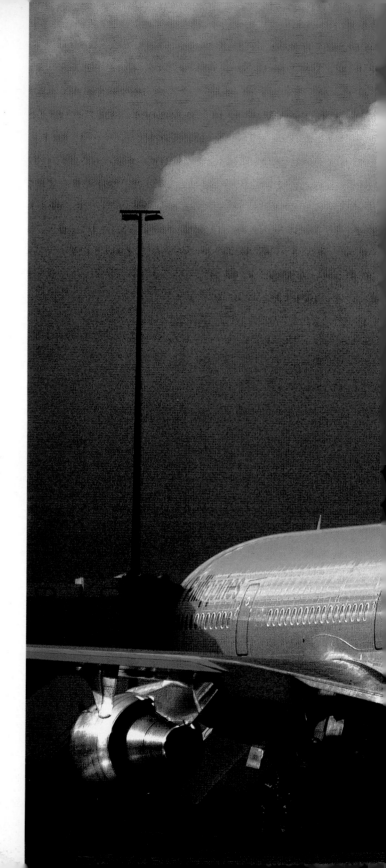

Philippine Airlines' striking new livery
symbolizes the new era of democracy being
enjoyed by the country it serves. This DC-10
is visiting Melbourne

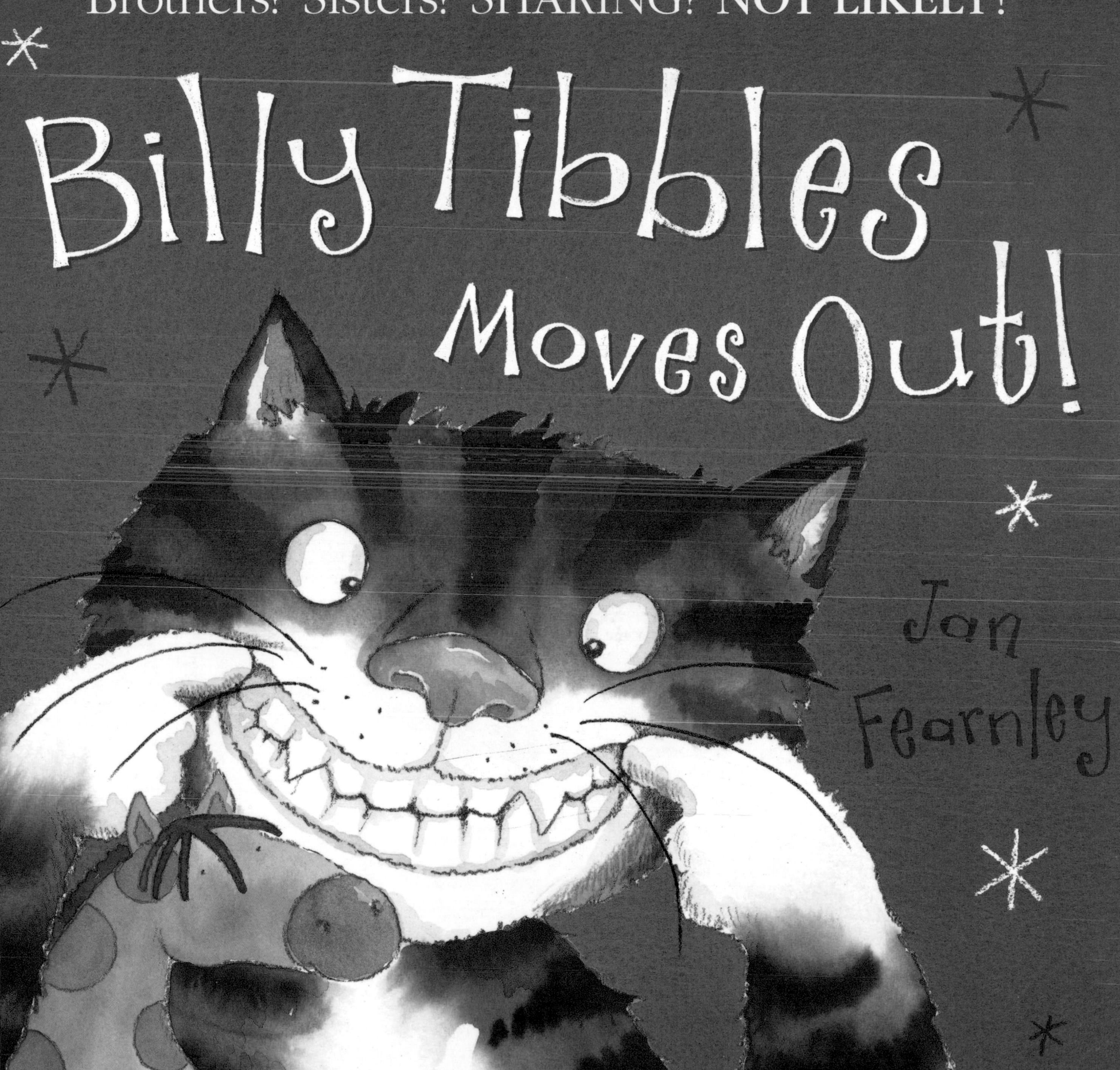

Brothers? Sisters? SHARING? NOT LIKELY!

Billy Tibbles Moves Out!

Jan Fearnley

WHERE THE CLOCK STANDS STILL

TO

Jim, Wendy, Jock,
Robbie and Fiona.

DOWN TO THE SEA AGAIN

All roads lead to the sea. Each of the East Neuk villages has its wynds running down from the high ground to the shore, but Pittenweem's are the steepest and finest. Many a fisherman's feet have swung down here to the boats and back again, heavy with tiredness or springing with the news of a bumper catch.

SCHOOL WYNDE, PITTENWEEM, SEPTEMBER 1987.

WHERE THE CLOCK STANDS STILL

A Portrait of
the East Neuk of Fife

CLIFF WILSON
Words by Christopher Rush

CANONGATE

First published in 1990 by Canongate Publishing
16 Frederick Street, Edinburgh EH2 2HB

Photographs © Cliff Wilson 1990
Introduction and Captions © Christopher Rush 1990

British Library Cataloguing in Publication Data
Wilson, Cliff
Where the clock stands still: the East Neuk of Fife.
1. Scotland. Fife Region. Social life
I. Title
941.290858

ISBN 0-86241-303-6

Typeset by Hewer Text Composition Services
Printed and bound by Butler and Tanner, Frome

CONTENTS

ACKNOWLEDGEMENTS

IT IS DIFFICULT to single out particular people from amongst those who have been kind enough to help me prepare the material for this book, but it would take a separate volume to mention them all.

I must therefore make special mention of the following for their technical assistance and kind words of encouragement: Robbie Pollock and staff at Ardross Farm, Harry Thomson and family at St Ford's Farm, Alex Macleod, Factor of Elie Estates, Hamish Lohoar and Tom at Drumcarro Farm, Dave Wilson and Family, Farriers; Stephen and Carol Grieve, Potters of Crail, John Reekie, golfclub maker, Geoff Squires, artist, Dr Jo Simpson of East Neuk Ltd, Calum MacDonald of P.T.S. Ltd; Jim Wood and the crew of 'Launch Out', Jock Wood and the crew of 'Minnie Wood II', Willie Miller and Dave Anderson of 'Guide Us', Willie Gay and the crew of 'Constant Hope', John Watson and the staff of Christie Marine, Billy Hughes and the staff of the Fishermen's Mutual Assoc., the directors and staff of Miller Yard, St Monans, Officer in Charge H.M. Coastguard Crail, Sandy Black, Elie Sailing Club, Jim Lindsay and staff of Scottish Fisheries Museum, Anstruther Crail, and of course my family for putting up with me during this period. Finally, I am immensely grateful to Christopher Rush for his kindness in supplying captions and an Introduction to my photographs.

FRONT COVER PHOTOGRAPH

Fergie. I will always hold this photograph in special affection. I took it the first time that I met Fergie, when he was mending nets at the end of Pittenweem pier on a warm but misty day. Although now retired, Fergie still helps out occasionally with net mending. However, in his heyday he was a deep sea fisherman, and has many a story to tell.

PITTENWEEM, MARCH 1987.

PREFACE

THE PEOPLE OF the East Neuk live in communities based around the six main villages of Elie, St Monans, Pittenweem, Anstruther, Cellardyke and Crail. The way they make their living, whether from the land or the sea, and their customs and traditions have remained virtually unchanged for generations.

I have wanted to record this way of life for a long time. There are no other contemporary photographic records of these communities whose undisturbed existences are now threatened by the invasion of commuters, tourists and modern priorities that the new road system being constructed will bring. To wait any longer would almost certainly have meant missing this important portion of Scottish life, and I feel that it is vital to capture it in an accurate visual record before it has vanished forever.

My family has long had connections with the East Neuk, and when I was a schoolboy I used to help the local fisherman, Jimmy Linton, pull up his lobster creels aboard his boat 'Trusty'. It was during this period that my love of the sea and the area began, and the seeds for this book were sown.

Although my employment took me to many countries all over the world my heart stayed in the East Neuk, until eventually the call was too great, and I had to return.

After I qualified as a photographer my thoughts turned once more to the possibility of this book. My first plan was to complete the gathering of the material alongside my commercial assignments, but I soon found that the subject was so absorbing that there was no option but to devote my whole time to the project, which has taken me three and a half years to complete. During this period I have tried to adopt the 'fly on the wall' approach, to try and give a true picture of life, and to this end the vast majority of the photographs were shot on very fast film and in atrocious weather conditions. I've been wet, cold and often fed up at myself; handed steaming-hot mugs of tea by a man with hands that could swallow the mug, and pulled to my feet on a heaving deck by a fisherman with a great smile; shared that final moment before the calf is born with the stockman, or had a few words with the combine harvester driver whilst he pushed through the night to meet Mother Nature's deadline.

Now the task has been completed I can look back on the many friends I have made and the happy times we have shared together, such as the time I saw old Jimmy Sharkey mending a dry stane dyke as he has done year in year out, whilst traffic passed him by, oblivious to his presence.

Cliff Wilson

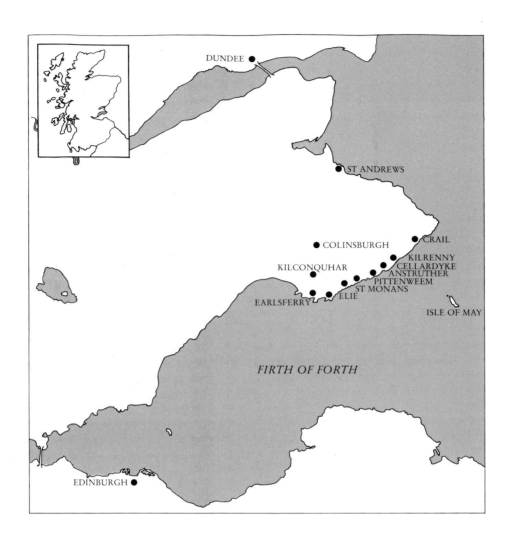

DUNDEE ●

ST ANDREWS ●

● COLINSBURGH   ● CRAIL

                                   ● KILRENNY
KILCONQUHAR ●   ● CELLARDYKE
                              ● ANSTRUTHER
                        ● PITTENWEEM
                  ● ST MONANS
EARLSFERRY ● ● ELIE

                              ISLE OF MAY

FIRTH OF FORTH

EDINBURGH ●

INTRODUCTION

SOME YEARS AGO I tried to persuade a well known professional photographer to work with me on a book of pictures of the East Neuk. I even tramped about Fife in advance, making extensively detailed notes towards the collection I hoped would result. It never did. The photographer quoted as his fee more than I earned in a year and assured me that this would be required 'up front'. I dropped the idea and threw away my notes.

So it was with immediately rekindled interest and enthusiasm that I heard, in the spring of this year, that a collection of contemporary photographs by Cliff Wilson was to appear, located in the East Neuk, and that the publishers wanted me to provide the words. My secondary reaction was annoyance—that I had shredded my notes for the book unborn. That act of destruction had been carried out in one of those moments of depressed frustration, when a writer feels that the practicalities of communicating an idea to the public are just too hard to overcome and that very probably the idea would never have worked anyway.

As soon as I saw Cliff Wilson's pictures my irritation vanished. Like all works of art they recreate an experience entirely, rendering redundant any ideas and emotions which might have attached to that experience before you saw the actual picture. Images spawn images; my own mind works by image rather than by analysis, building up verbal picture blocks from life. Exposed to these photographs, new words flooded my mind: I saw Fife all over again, realising that you can experience a place for nearly five decades without ever knowing it completely.

This book is a reflection of the infinite oyster that the East Neuk is: open it and you will find yourself looking at new pearls, formed from the grit of living. I hope that my own appreciation of these pearls, in words, may act as a little glass wherein the reader will see the inmost parts of them and come away the richer, the wiser.

Even should I fail, each picture in itself is worth a thousand words.

Fife.

A Danish word originally—at least according to one of its historians of antiquity, the scholar Sibbald, who tells us (let us achieve a willing suspension of disbelief for the moment) that it means 'the wooded country', from the word *fibhe*, of course! It has to be said that another derivation goes back to the cotton-grass that once waved upon the Fife marshes. And other linguists undo the locks of other words, teasing us out of thought. I rather like the idea of the wooded country.

But why Danish?

You only have to look at Fife on the map of Scotland to see why. The Kingdom thrusts itself into the North Sea (the German Ocean as it used to be called) like the head of a belligerent wolf, challenging the snarling longships to come and have a bash.

As come they did. To Fifeness, the muzzle of the hound, where Fifemen waited, and where the Danes' Dyke and the Longman's Grave record their incursions; to the May Island, where 6000 monks were massacred (a scribal exaggeration of one zero too many, perhaps?); and to the Caiplie Coves, Crail, St Monans, and all along the coast to Earlsferry, where stone coffins were unearthed containing their remains. In fact the Danish Vikings met with so many defeats in Fife that it came to be known as their burial ground. The crafty sea-wolves were given something to think about by the craftier Fifers.

And why the wooded country? Well, that was a long time ago. When King James IV built his naval *pièce de résistance*, 'The Great Michael', it was said that he had all the woods in Fife cut down for the purpose. Another exaggeration, naturally. But Fife was where his cutters first came, with keel-searching axes, as indeed so many famed figures from history trooped across the kingdom and passed through the East Neuk, leaving their stories in the places that remain.

It was in Fife that Alexander III plunged to his death; Macduff fled from Macbeth; Malcolm met Margaret; Robert the Bruce's parents courted at Kilconquhar; Mary of Guise-Lorraine landed at Balcomie, remarking on the striking looks of the Scottish women as soon as her feet touched Scottish soil; Sir Andrew Wood trounced the flower of Henry VIII's navy between Crail and the May Island; Alexander Selkirk (alias Robinson Crusoe) sailed from Largo; the survivors of the Spanish Armada put in to Anstruther and were well treated; the notorious bloody Beaton was slung into a forgotten grave near Kilrenny; James V crossed the Dreel Burn on the back of a gaberlunzie girl; and as the Spenses were Constables of Crail in the thirteenth century, I rather fancy—in spite of an Aberdeenshire school of preference—that it was on an East Neuk strand that the good Sir Patrick Spens was walking when he received the fatal royal mandate to cross the sea to Norway.

Things are tougher than we are. The people have gone: the places still stand. And something else lingers on—an aura of that rich historical heritage that has permeated the very stones of the sea-caves where the first East Neuk hermits hung out, Stone Age man sighted whales, monks saw mermaids, and desperadoes and drop-outs lived out their ruined and eccentric lives beside the crash of waves.

Waves.

It is the sound of the sea that dominates the East Neuk. I was born and bred in St Monans, whose burgh motto, inscribed beneath a picture of some men in a boat, reads *Mare vivimus*: we live by the sea. To a community of fishers and boatbuilders these words encapsulated a philosophy as well as a fact of life: the sea is everything; the sea is god. Brought into a world that was noisy with gulls, bright with the running tide, ecstatic with kippers and tar, it was impossible for me to escape the sway of the omnipresent sea, even if I had wanted to.

Its glintings and whisperings were everywhere, even inland on a quiet day. And on not so quiet days it came in like a maniac, a maker of momentary white castles, crashing into the harbours, dislodging the huge sarsens of the piers with a power that would have made Stonehenge topple like a pack of cards. I soon learned to respect it and to respect the fishermen who danced with death every day on the sea's changing face, always in danger of disappearing down its white throat. Whenever that happened a chill struck the community, harder than frost, colder than marble on the kiryard hill.

My own village kirk is dedicated to St Monan, the local saint who was martyred on the May Island one Dark Age day, according to one tradition. It stands closest to the sea of any church in Scotland and in heavy weathers I used to watch the waves climbing the graveyard walls, wetting the latticed windows, spraying the lichened tombs of my forebears.

Inside the church and high in the vaulted roof, one of these ancestors had placed there for me a vivid reminder of that ancient connection between the scriptures and the sea. Fishing is an act of faith and a highly dangerous occupation and so seafarers have always been superstitious at the very least and deeply religious at best. My great-great-great-great-uncle, Captain Marr, a native of St Monans, captained a 130-gun frigate during the time of the Napoleonic naval engagements and his ship acquitted itself so well that it earned some prize money. The bounty was never collected, however, because by the time it was paid over the crew had dispersed. With the gold Captain Marr therefore decided to commission a replica of his vessel, which he then gifted to St Monans church. It still holds literal sway over the pulpit, symbol of those godfearing men that went down to the waters to do business in great ships, the very names of the local fishing boats pointing the connection: *The Shepherd Lad, The Magdalene, The True Vine.*

And all along the coastline and down the firth the steeples of the other village churches speared the sky, pointing to God all the year round and especially on Sundays; beckoning the boats home. The fishermen soon found a practical use, though, for the towers of God. When fishing just offshore they used the kirk spires in conjunction with certain other objects to enable them to take a bearing on the land and so pinpoint precisely a favoured fishing ground for lobsters or fish. This was known as 'taking a meads' and brought up full creels and nets in the days before silicon chips and echo sounders. The most distinctive hill between Elie and Anstruther is Kellie Law. Hence 'Kellie ower the kirks' was one such line-up and the chimneys on certain houses were similarly used, easily identifiable on their crow-stepped gables to the practised eye, probing the clutter of red pantiled roofs that jostled down to each of the harbours.

When I was a boy these harbours glittered with herring and haddocks and flounders and cod: a miracle of the sea's bounty, so it seemed to me, as I stood on the braehead at St Monans, looking down over the rooftops, through a white net of gulls, at the scene far beneath my feet: the boats coming in, the hardy fishermen with just a few spars of wood between them and the prancing white bull of the sea; the piers littered with fish-scales that caught the sun and broke it up a billion times, a scattering of bright coins in the busy mornings; and the buyers shouting like evangelists, the battle for the fish transferred now from the sea to the economic arena of the market; while all around me the air rang with the clubbing sounds of the hammers on wood as Miller's boatbuilders laboured like Jonahs in the ribs of their great wooden whales, spawned by peace and necessity, yet more boats to catch more fish to buy more loaves and so keep the age of miracles afloat.

Naturally I thought that I was in heaven and that paradise would have no ending. I cannot recall a day when I knew that Eden was almost over but the last steam drifter left the East Neuk for the East Anglian fishing grounds in 1956, when I was twelve and before I was out of my teens the Firth of Forth was a blue graveyard, each wave the wind-tossed epitaph of a drowned tradition.

With the emptying of the harbours came the emptying of many of the houses and shops. Young men and women moved away to find work elsewhere and retired people from the towns and cities moved in. Recently I visited a St Monans that had no chemist, no cobbler, no butcher, no barber, and—most incredibly—no fish-and-chip-shop! A ghost town to what it once was.

There were other losses too. Every kind of advance involves some form of recession and the undoubted advantages of the Forth Road bridge in 1964, the increase of cars on the road, the easy availability of televisions and videos, all played their part in the killing of the local worthies. Centuries of hard work, grinding poverty, isolation and close living create eccentricity. Mild-mannered cranks peopled my boyhood as they still inhabit my memory: a breeder of snails, a drowner of cats, a preacher to seagulls; an aspiring suicide who kept changing his mind and had to be rescued from the harbour; and an old gold-earringed, white-bearded sailor of ninety who gave me a line I managed to make famous: 'I've seen monsoons and typhoons and baboons and teaspoons!' When he whispered these words fiercely to me in the street one day by the boatyard I was less than five years old.

It is said that fishermen have but one master but actually they have two: the sea and their wives. At least that is the way it used to be and if the East Neuk is no longer quite such a matriarchal society, it is nonetheless the female worthies I remember best. One of them who would never wash and smelt to heaven was made decent for the pews by the old gravedigger and beadle, Ecky Feggy in popular parlance. He stripped her down bare buff, laid her out like a corpse on a fishmonger's slab in his back garden, adjoining the kirk, and washed her, back, belly and in between. His whole thought on cleanliness, he performed this as an act of charity, serving the church with hose and scrubbing brush to the glory of God and the fury of the Woman's Guild.

Another old lady, an aunt twice great, fed me hellfire and pandrops, began my literary education by quoting Tennyson to me and my sex education by telling me that boys came from the Bass Rock and girls from the May Island. She was dead before I was three—a figure which shows the impression she made on me.

All of them did; who salted the earth with the tang of their talk and traditions and stories. It was an age of storytelling and I liked nothing better than to stand by the harbour walls and watch the old retired fishermen walking up and down at the corner. In a bunch of twelve usually they gathered there each morning, clad in navy blues, blacks, greys and browns; coarse-trousered, guernseyed, jacketed and cheese-cutter capped, they took out their pipes and passed the stories round from mouth to remembering mouth like a pitcher; stories of sharks and storms and witches and whales and giant skates.

And as they talked they walked incessantly. Twelve steps to the west, from the corner; twelve steps to the east, back to the corner, their old shoes pacing the length of an imaginary deck, according to a rhythm that retirement could not erase. An occasional spit over a ghostly gunwale into a sea they had left years ago, and so it went on all the day: twelve steps and turn, twelve steps and turn, the disciples of a vanished fishing culture, a string of old kippers, land-locked penguins that had seen better days, filling the air with tobacco and talk and my young head with the stories I was later to record for posterity, though I never knew it at the time.

My seatown home was, for my first two decades of life, the centre of a universe whose outer rim stretched as far as Kilconquhar and Cellardyke, a radius of little more than two or three miles in any given direction, except for the sea. Across the water, blue with distance, the May Island and the Bass Rock were fabled continents and Berwick Law was on the other side of the world. Each of the villages along the golden fringe of Fife possessed its own characteristic flavour. St Monans revelled in its ten churches for a thousand souls: Church of Scotland, Congregationalists, Salvation Army, Catholics (who were Irish and went to Pittenweem), Open Brethren, Close Brethren, Fergusson's Brethren, Duff's Brethren, the Pilgrims—and foot-washing baptists of a persuasion whose precise theologies I have forgotten, if I ever knew. Not surprisingly St Monans was known throughout the East Neuk as The Holy City! Elie was the home of the gentry, Anstruther folk were more sociable than Pittenweemers, the Crailers were a quiet breed of men. As for Cellardyke, it was the home both of the most intrepid line fishermen in the country and the quirkiest clutch of worthies that roamed the coastline close to their own homes.

To each of the fishing havens a different motto. That of St Monans, *Mare Vivimus*, I have already described. Underneath these words were another two: *Grip Fast*—inciting the sea-bull-dogs of the Holy City to watch both their seafaring and spiritual step. Bible-boatmen that they were, they mostly did. And so did the men of the neighbouring burghs, following their mottoes from Elie to Fifeness, guided on coats-of-arms by bishops and oarsmen and stars.

Perhaps the words that stick fastest in my mind are those that comprise the motto of Cellardyke, inscribed beneath a seal showing five men in a boat, letting down into the sea an enormous hook, medieval with unperspective: *Semper tibi pendeat hamus:* May you always have a hook in the water. (Or, if you are no Sassenach and can speak the local lingo: May ye aye hae a heuk in the watter!) Whether in Latin, English or Scots, the words carry a tough optimism that acknowledges the dominance of the sea.

Indeed the East Neuk is often thought of merely as a maritime scattering of peoples. But its fishing townships are strung out like pearls along a line of rich farmlands that wester away well beyond Kellie Law, the single hill to which I lifted mine eyes when I was not looking at the water. The old hostilities between farm and fisherfolk that once caused pitched battles in St Monans (the grappling iron versus the hayfork, with herds of pigs sent out like cavalry to head the farmers' charge) have shaded these days into friendly and ironic banter. At school, certainly, we thought of the farm boys as a race apart, creatures of dung and clay as opposed to tar and tangle. Nowadays it is easier to see the ties that bind rather than the elements that divide, as both farmer and fisherman face the common nightmare of political and economic pressures, forces that grow steadily stronger and less predictable than wind and tide, snowfall and frost, flooding and drought.

The photographs in this book are a reminder to me of the many facets of life in the East Neuk I have just described—but such vivid reminders are they that they present themselves with the force of fresh experience, revelation, incarnation. It is as such, capturing the spirit and not just the bones of the place, that they go beyond the merely photographic. For a photograph which is nothing more than a photograph is simply a *copy* of reality: something that has come out of a machine, not a mind. At the other end of the artistic spectrum are the paintings of the masters: pictures that are not copies but *illusions* of reality; selections from experience which break up on analysis into bits and blobs of light but which cohere in a way that says something of significance about places, about people. A great photograph, in its recreation rather than merely passive imitation of experience, partakes of the speaking power of the master's canvas.

And the photographs of Cliff Wilson speak whole volumes in folio. They tell of the three-ply twine of East Neuk life: the two toils of land and sea and the secret lives of the hard-shelled communities in between. They reveal a subsoil of history, a submerged heritage, pulsating beneath the spare flesh of the present: the blue skin of the firth, the green skin of the farms.

What is especially striking about them is that nothing in them stays still: everything is on the move. The hands and heads of men, white heads, young heads, are active all the time and their bodies aligned to the movements of waves and beasts, the heavings of fields and sea. The human movements may vary with the modern machinery of milking and hauling and harvesting and ploughing, but certain elements remain constant: the wear and tear on hands, the backbending sweat of labour; patience, precision, insight, endurance; the qualities of men that must suffer everything under and including the sun.

Even the very houses are not asleep; they move too. Or rather the art of Cliff Wilson makes them move: from the seagulled chimney tops down past the pantiled roofs and crowstepped gables to the windings of the tide, splashing the doorsteps of the shore-facing streets. To a Jeremiah like myself, living in Edinburgh and lamenting my own exile from Eden, the loss of innocence, these pictures are not poignant but positive. They teach me a lesson: life is still going on: an extremely hard and active life—in Pittenweem, in the North Sea, in the inland farms and homesteads. The mending of nets and the making of pottery are skills as old as history. Everywhere you can see eyes intent on the work of the hands: a golf club, a horseshoe, a lobster pot, a winch.

This book exposes the skeleton of the past but clothes it with the flesh of the present which you would not know is there, unless you have walked the earth

THREE IN ONE

From the summit of Kellie Law the trinity of East Neuk life may be seen: farmlands and sea, and the villages, Cellardyke and Anstruther, in between. The spire of Chalmers Memorial Church juts into the white horses that fleck the firth, while on the skyline, swept by rain and mist, rises the May Island. Now the home of thousands of seabirds, a colony of monks were once shut in on its beetling crags, their psalms and masses accompanied by the rattling shackles of the sea.

KELLIE LAW, MARCH 1990.

and sailed the sea at ungodly hours, as Cliff Wilson has done. Correction: they are not ungodly hours; they are the very times in which you will meet your maker, if you are wise: in the birth of a calf, the breath of a barley stalk, the wings of a bird keeping time with your keel.

The unity of being is here too: the tractor trails gulls like the fishing boat, unearthing the fish, salvaging the worm from the earth-wave for the same ravenous beak; the trawler digs the blue ploughlands of the firth; the helmsman harvester sits alone on a stubble sea. There are no old rivalries worth the effort: there is only man against the elemental thrust of life. Houses grow out of the rocks; commanding skies stand over sweeps of stubble, tracts of sea, crenellations of churches and chimneys and crags. The kirk spires conduct the symphonies of clouds and water, light and shade; the seatown dances on the waves.

Look at these pictures, reader, and be wise. The world is still beautiful; Eden is not a dream; there *is* a green and pleasant land; and Jerusalem is with us now. And not far away. Would that we could keep it that way. The world, unfortunately, is on a self-destruct course. Should the beauty of the East Neuk ever disappear, this book at least will help us to remember that such things were.

Christopher Rush.
2nd April 1990, EDINBURGH.

THE VILLAGES

THE PULSE OF LIFE in the East Neuk is to be felt at its strongest in the six main coastal villages of Elie, St Monans, Pittenweem, Anstruther, Cellardyke and Crail and the hard fact of life that binds them together is best epitomised by the burgh motto of St Monans: *Mare vivimus:* we live by the sea. To find the inner spirit of these fishing townships, however, we should look to the motto of the Cellardykers: *Semper tibi pendeat hamus:* May you always have a hook in the water. Here is both a hardy optimism and a stern acknowledgement of the element and calling on which they all depended at one time for their very existence.

In spite of these common ties, the villages maintained for generations a set of fierce rivalries in the jealous guardianship of their own individual traditions, talk, customs and methods of work. In turn the fishing people of each port kept up a traditional hostility against the farming folk from inland and the nether towns, particularly in St Monans, where pitched battles took place between the two. A fisher lass would never have married a ploughman: nor would marriages have occurred between one village and another.

Centuries of such close living produced a race apart in each of the havens: a colourful race of men and women, their traditionally appointed Christian names—and surnames common as daisies—so confusing that men were distinguished from their namesakes by the names of their boats: Acorn Peter, Dawn Peter, Venus Peter.

Gone are the old salts who pursued the silver darlings; they are sleeping now under lichened tombs in the sea-splashed kirkyards, where the steeples act as landmarks for the few boats that still come and go with the tides. Insularity and superstition have largely disappeared, but so, alas, has work: the fish have moved away, the boatbuilding is confined to a single yard and tourism is taking over as a source of employment and revenue. The worthies and eccentrics have vanished too, the storytelling and folk wisdom, the lore and lure of a string of communities that remained fossilised for centuries only to lose their character in the last decades of the present millennium.

CASTLES OF THE FOAM

Houses, harbours, kirks, castle and doocot present an embattled frontage to the misty Firth of Forth, defending the peoples of the sea against the incursions of time and the elements. Looking westward from Pittenweem to St Monans, the salient features on the crenellated skyline are the round tower of the old salt pans, frowning like some fortified broch on the brow of the cliff, and the stubby finger of the Old Kirk of St Monan, linking land, sea and sky.

WEST OF PITTENWEEM, JANUARY 1990.

THE CALL OF THE RUNNING TIDE

Untouched as yet by the salt and seaweeds of another season, the spruce pleasure boats of
Elie Sailing Club are lifted into the water at low tide.

ELIE HARBOUR, JULY 1987.

HEAVY WEATHER

And the flung spray, and the blown spume, and the seagulls crying.

The stormy Firth of Forth hits Elie harbour with a ferocity that makes you feel for the fisherman, facing such wind and wave. The old granary glowers defiantly, clothed with the flung spray.

ELIE, JANUARY 1988.

ANOTHER TIME ANOTHER PLACE

Cupped in the palm of the surrounding countryside, Kilconquhar looks as if it had been wafted inland by a thoughtful tidal wave of long ago and then left to itself. The most peaceful retreat in the area, its cathedral-like church tower beckons the traveller to what could easily be mistaken for a quaint old English village.

KILCONQUHAR VILLAGE, SEPTEMBER 1987.

A PRIVATE CLUB

So many of the solitary skills have now vanished and you can no longer watch the coopers and sailmakers of Fife at work in the seatown shops and yards. Yet here, as John Reekie plies his quiet trade, you catch a splinter from the past. The last of a long line of golfmakers in the East Neuk, John carried on his father's tradition until he retired and now makes and repairs clubs for the favoured few.

EARLSFERRY, BACK GARDEN OF JOHN REEKIE'S WORKSHOP, MAY 1988.

THE SMIDDY

The country smiddies are now melancholy. In its heyday this humble-seeming cottage throbbed with life. Inside the smith lived among sparks, brushing them off like bees, while his bellows blew noisily, the smoke from the chimneys feathering the surrounding sky.

COLINSBURGH, 1987.

CROWSTEPS

Looking eastwards over the crow-stepped gables and pantiled roofs of St Monans that
jostle daftly down to the shore, you can see across the piers to Miller's boatyard, the last
fishing-boat building yard in the East Neuk and so its main employer. Boats have been
built here at Miller's since 1747, though keels have been ploughing the water since the men
of Stone Age St Monans took their first crow-steps into the firth.

ST MONANS, SEPTEMBER 1987.

HOUSEBOAT?

Mare vivimus is the burgh motto of St Monans: we live by the sea. This photograph provides a vivid illustration of that fact of life. The boat on the slipway almost seems to have left its element to mingle with the fisher cottages. Any closer and the prow will splinter the window panes!

MILLER'S SLIP, ST MONANS, NOVEMBER 1987.

WOODEN SHIPS AND IRON MEN

Inside one of the great wooden whales, we are looking into the curving ribs of the very last of the line of wooden-hulled boats to be built by Miller's of St Monans. The sylvan sound of the adze on wood is now replaced by the clang of metal in these days of steel hulls.

ST MONANS, NOVEMBER 1987.

WHERE ARE THE OLD TIMERS?

From the gull on the chimney top, down past the crowsteps to the outside stone stairs, this is a typical village scene in late autumn when the holiday crowds have gone. Only one vital element is sadly missing. Not so many years ago this corner was still the meeting point for the retired fishermen, who walked for hours up and down the pavement, smoking their pipes, telling their stories. Where are the old salts now?

WEST SHORE, ST MONANS, OCTOBER 1987.

ONWARD CHRISTIAN SAILORS

Although it hangs in the south transept, the ship in the picture appears to hover above the pulpit, a commanding symbol of the age-old connection between the scriptures and the sea. 'Onward, Christian sailors!' the bowsprit seems to say. This replica of his 130-gun frigate of the 18th century was gifted to the church by Captain Marr, a native of St Monans whose vessel had won prize money for its exploits in British naval engagements. By the time it was paid over, however, the crew had disbanded and so Captain Marr used the bounty to provide this handsome model, to the honour of seamen and the glory of God.

ST MONANS CHURCH, MARCH 1990.

29

THE HOLY CITY

Or so it was known throughout the East Neuk. The Old Kirk of St Monans heads and protects the village uncompromisingly. 'Wha daur meddle wi' me?' it seems to say, this ecclesiastical thistle whose squat head makes it the distinctive landmark of the entire area. The 'murder-holes' in the tower (arrows were fired from these slits in times of invasion) confirm the impression of impregnable dourness. Perched on a green wave of graves, this church stands closest to the sea of any in the country and in the winter its lichened tombs are splashed with brine.

WEST OF ST MONANS, MARCH 1990.

30

OLD SAILORS NEVER DIE

In St Monans, at any rate, the fishermen always stay close to their element, even in the green wave of the kirkyard hill. The tombstones of these old salts are often laced with spray and in heavy weathers wetted by waves. Here at least a crew comes safely into harbour. Many of the East Neuk headstones tell a different story—of boats gone down in storms and sometimes scores of children orphaned by a single sea.

OLD KIRK, ST MONANS, MARCH 1990.

31

SPACE AGE CAVE

This ancient formation, an accident of prehistory, looks like a set which an avant garde director might have laboured to design for a production of *Macbeth* or *Siegfried* on the contemporary stage. St Fillan's Cave, Pittenweem, is one of a number of East Neuk 'steddis' or sea-caves, once inhabited by monks and hermits, lunatics, criminals and all kinds of political and psychological drop-outs from society. Now the property of the Church, this cave must at one time have been the best living accommodation that the East Neuk could provide.

ST FILLANS, PITTENWEEM, MARCH 1990.

STANDS THE CHURCH CLOCK

And is there honey still for tea?

With headscarf and shopping bags in Pittenweem. Women and the church still dominate life in these matriarchal and godfearing communities.

PITTENWEEM, MARCH 1990.

32

33

BACK TO THE FUTURE

A handful of clues as to the historical period in which this picture is shot, including the registration plate on the car, of course. Remove that alien-seeming handful and you could step back two centuries. And more. Routin Row is a corruption of *route de roi* or 'king's way' and it is not hard to picture Charles II coming round the corner.

ROUTIN ROW, PITTENWEEM, AUGUST 1987.

WHITINGS

Shining whitely in the sunlight, the houses of the West Shore, like those of Routin Row,
would defy you to date the picture—but for the tell-tale street lamps. Now occupied by
holidayers and the retired, these were once the dwellings of the skippers and salts of the
Pittenweem fishing fleet. The sea splashed their very doorsteps.

PITTENWEEM, AUGUST 1987.

35

A WELL KNOWN MEADS

The needling spire of Chalmers Memorial Church dominates this sea symphony of light and shade. For generations local fishermen used the distinctive steeples of the East Neuk to enable them to take a 'meads' or bearing on the land, and to locate favoured fishing grounds offshore. Thus the canny skippers found a good practical use for religion!

ANSTRUTHER, MARCH 1990.

A STAR IN THE EAST

The inevitable clutter of crowsteps and chimney pots leads the eye past the sea-girt windings and out to the humble lighthouse. Hardly larger looking than a lum itself, the star for seamen is nevertheless very necessary to the men of Pittenweem.

EAST SHORE, PITTENWEEM, AUGUST 1987.

COIL THE ROPES ON SHORE

So ran the refrain of the old fishing song from the days when the clinker-built cutters
pushed out from Scottish harbours, casting white nets in the winter, black nets in summer.
Only several spars of wood between the fisherman and the sea, but they were put together
with such tough grace—the curving lines of the boat built without draught plans—by the
rule-of-thumb and keen-eyed shipwrights, that they shrugged off the dashing waves and
brought their sailors safely home.

SCOTTISH FISHERIES MUSEUM, ANSTRUTHER, MARCH 1990.

LEVIATHAN

Canst thou open the doors of his face? Canst thou draw out leviathan with an hook?

From Cellardyke's whaling station many men set out for the Davis Straits. Captain William Smith sailed with the Leith fleet and brought back to his home in Cellardyke the jawbone of the biggest whale ever taken in the Arctic seas. He set it up as it stands today—the most imposing entrance to the *back* of a house one could hope to see!

EAST FORTH STREET, CELLARDYKE, MARCH 1990.

39

DRIVE WITH CARE

Cellardyke's narrow streets have always contained the impetuous spirits of drivers. The chariots of Jehu may have passed this way, but the experienced tourist will hire a man with a red flag to precede him along this last undeveloped area. Notice the marriage lintel above the doorway on the left.

CELLARDYKE, MARCH 1990.

UNTOLD ON STONE

Thomas Watson, a local fisherman, was press-ganged in Cellardyke in 1799 along with his wife, Mary Buek, taken because she was a nurse. Watson rose to the rank of bosun gunner and their daughter Margaret was born on board HMS *Ardent* during the bombardment of Copenhagen in 1801. At the age of $4^1/_2$ she was with her parents on board Nelson's flagship, the *Victory*, during the battle of Trafalgar, and as a old lady of ninety could still remember snatches of the famous engagement! Thomas and Mary Watson returned to Cellardyke where they kept an ale-and-pie shop at the harbour head. With typical East Neuk understatement Watson's gravestone describes him simply as 'Mariner, Cellardyke'!

KILRENNY KIRKYARD, NEAR CELLARDYKE, MARCH 1990.

THE BULWARK

Cellardyke Harbour at the end of winter, looking eastwards to the area known as The Bulwark. When the drier weather arrives in April, the clothes poles along the rickety pier will be flagged with billowing white sails as the local women hang out their washing in the bright spring winds.

CELLARDYKE, MARCH 1990.

A CHARMED CIRCLE

The enfolding arms of Crail Harbour crook protectively round its handful of boats. Safe
within the cradling piers, the small craft that remain are mostly devoted to the crab and
lobster trade. Here is the most protected haven in the East Neuk.

CRAIL HARBOUR, MARCH 1990.

LET THE LOWER LIGHTS BE BURNING

Thy word is a lamp unto my feet and a light unto my path.

The boat comes into Crail by day, but on dirty nights the two red navigation lights would be an indispensable beacon for skippers to line their helms upon in the approach to harbour.

CRAIL, MARCH 1990.

44

THE WORK OF THE WHEEL

One of the oldest trades practised by human hands, those of Stephen and Carol Grieve
work hard during the winter to ensure a well-stocked pottery for the summer tourists.

CRAIL POTTERY, FEBRUARY 1986.

45

THE LAND

THE PASTORAL MYTH is as old as history, the Genesis story of the Garden of Eden being one of the first accounts of a world in which nature was kind to unfallen man and the earth was idyllic, without original sin. But for centuries afterwards people continued to believe, or to pretend to believe, that the countryside was a peaceful place to live, free from worries, free from toil. The pictures in this section reveal the truth of the matter: that the country is not a pastoral paradise but a place where man must earn his bread—and make it—by the sweat of his brow.

Most farmers are not, according to popular fable, up with the lark: they are up with the owl! By 4 am they will be seeing to the cows and their first milking, that is if they have not been up even earlier with the stockmen and shepherds at calving and lambing times, helping the beasts through difficult births, tending the younglings in their first precarious dawns.

Then there are the fields and their crops to work on and worry over, sowing and harvesting, through the ancient anxieties of weather and the newer problems caused by the breakdown of machines. First the chilly spring pricks through, then the waves of growth go over the land: the green wave of summer, the yellow wave of autumn, the brown wave of ploughing, the white wave of winter. The farmer turns in for a brief spell of rest and thinks again of the year to come. A far cry from heaven.

And yet, when you compare life in these photographs with the squalid, frenzied hubbubs of the stockmarkets and the unreal cities, where man is divorced from the creation, you may indeed argue that here indeed is heaven on earth, the old Elysium: *et in Arcadia ego.*

> *Let other folk make money faster*
> *In the air of dark-roomed towns;*
> *I don't dread a peevish master,*
> *Though no man may heed my frowns.*

THE BIG SKY

Only a man harrowing clods . . .

It is difficult not to think here of the novels and poems of Thomas Hardy. But whether in nineteenth century Wessex or contemporary Fife some things never alter; and whether by line fisherman or hoe-bearing farmer, patience and toil continue to be practised.

ARDROSS FARM, MARCH 1990.

49

SPRING PLOUGHING

The keel thrusts deeply into the field for the spring potato planting and the earth turns over like water in rich dark waves. In October the land will be wounded again for the picking. To the wave-blooms, out on the firth, there comes no autumn, but the ploughing and harvesting of the sea continues all the year round.

ARDROSS FARM, MARCH 1990.

BORN AMONG STRAW

Mother and child in an ageless nativity scene.

GIBBLESTON FARM, MARCH 1988.

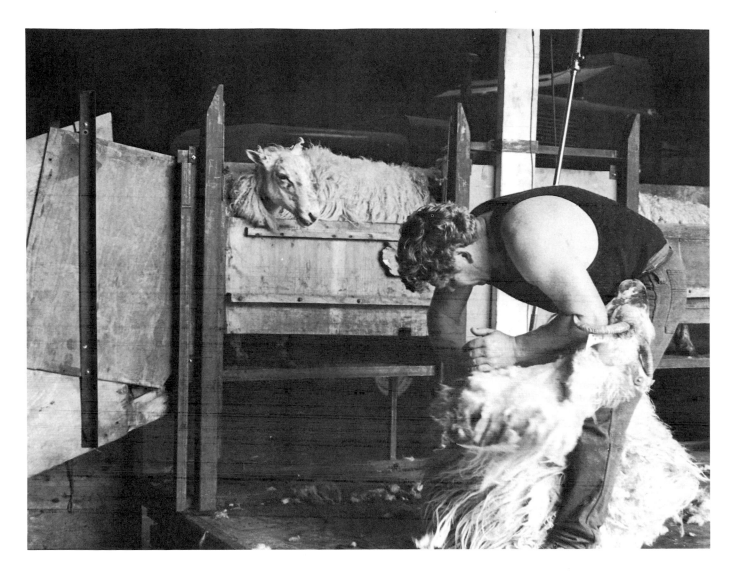

THE GOLDEN FLEECE

Undeterred by the scimitar-like horn hooked into his bare flesh, Robbie Pollock, head shearer at Ardross Farm, bends to his task, with hands that seem capable of wrestling a ram. The next sheep looks on with an appraising if somewhat wary eye.

ARDROSS FARM, ELIE, APRIL 1987.

THE FIRST CUT

Hamish Lohoar shearing the first of his flock. Modern machinery may have taken much of the labour out of the old clipping method, but the backbreaking toil of the countryman's existence is one factor which stays constant. Fortunately for Hamish the new belt provides welcome support in this most tiresome of trades.

DRUMCARRO FARM, MAY 1989.

UP THE LINE TO DIP
Spring and autumn bring the sheep to the dreaded dipping. The chemicals used to kill the termites may change but the men's task remains the same—to persuade a grass-going bundle of mutton and wool to take to the water, however briefly.

ARDROSS FARM, APRIL 1988.

55

ARDROSS OR ARDENNES?

Remove the rolls of fencing and you could be looking at the outbuildings of a Continental monastery or medieval vineyard. Horsegear once jingled in these cool vaults, while up aloft lay mountains of stored grain. Now the general clutter looks strangely at odds with the weathered classicality of the ancient arches.

ARDROSS FARM, JUNE 1987.

MILKING

The days of the dairymaid and the milking-stool have long gone, even from the East Neuk, but cows still need to be milked at an early hour, by whatever method the hardworking stockman pursues. Linden Butcher's work begins at 3 am. In addition to a busy day's labour, he must keep a meticulous record of each cow's yield of milk and calves. Seen here adjusting the flow from the bottle, he has the appearance more of a watchful precision surgeon than a farmer.

GIBBLESTON FARM, JULY 1988.

SHOPPING FOR SHOES
The shire horse has to be shod before the summer show season. This ton of white-faced docility can have a mind of its own at times and may prove a recalcitrant handful. The watchful dog has perhaps been made aware of this at some point!

THE SMITHY, BALMULLO, JUNE 1988.

IRONS IN THE FIRE

No more the smith his dusky brow shall clear,
Relax his ponderous strength and lean to hear.

But at Balmullo the blacksmith's trade has been handed down to Dave Wilson (a world
champion three times) by his farrier father. The numerical doodlings chalked up at his
back speak of more modern and technical matters, while he turns his attention meantime
to the oldest work of the anvil: the shoeing of heavy horses.

THE SMITHY, BALMULLO, APRIL 1987.

JOHN BARLEYCORN

Only reapers reaping early
In among the bearded barley

Only such early morning workers could hear the whispers etched against the sky in this lovely shot. Not that any of them would have the time to stop and listen before the white-bearded kings of the cornfield are cut down.

ST MONANS AREA, SEPTEMBER 1987.

THE EARL OF FIFE

A man's a man for a' that . . .

Sun and wind have weathered him for nearly seven decades till he seems a natural part of the land he never ceases to tend. One of the true Knights of the Fields, Jimmy Sharkey came over from Ireland as a boy in the 1920s and is now the last of the old drystane dykers left in the area.

ARDROSS FARM, MAY 1988.

60

A CORNER FOR CONSTABLE

Follow the St Monans burn backward from the sea to its source and you pass through sylvan scenes like these. Fife possibly takes its name from a Danish word meaning 'the wooded country' and it is said that when James IV built his prize ship *The Great Michael*, he felled every wood in Fife. Today's trees topple to less heroic purposes. This particular neck of the woods is one of the unspoiled corners of paradise.

NEAR COLINSBURGH, JUNE 1987.

MACHINES AND MEN

The last sighs of the corn as it is cut would not be heard by these reapers above the noise of their technology. They are much more intent on steering a parallel course so that the combine's load does not miss the trailer.

LOWER FIELDS, ARDROSS FARM, SEPTEMBER 1987.

63

STUBBLE BURNING

This takes place at the end of the harvest. Like all the other farmers, Harry Thompson Jr.
of St. Ford's farm is clearing his fields for the ploughing and sowing of next year's crop.
Throughout the East Neuk the late autumn evenings are fragrant with smoke and by night
the fields are flecked with the watch-fires of imaginary armies.

ST FORD'S FARM ELIE, SEPTEMBER 1987.

SHIP OF THE STUBBLE
Like a sturdy boat at sea, the tractor sits alone on a vast expanse of stubble field, the
solitary helmsman tuned in to Radio Scotland as he spreads lime on the field before it is
put to the plough.

ST FORD'S FARM, ELIE, SEPTEMBER 1987.

BROKEN WAVES

The seagulls flutter like a long bridal train in her wake, but she is wedded to her work in a ritual as old as the clay, this iron little lady of the land.

ST FORD'S FARM, SEPTEMBER 1987.

PLOUGHING

At Kincraig Point the 'farmship' thrusts into the field, forcing the land to behave like the sea, in taking on the wave-shapes of its huge 'propellers'. Donald Thomson has some difficult ground to plough here as the furrows churn like the sea.

ST FORD'S FARM, SEPTEMBER 1987.

DRESSING THE TROOPS

The October potato harvest calls for squads of casual labour, culled from the local populace to clear the fields for the occasion. Here however we see little shacks being shunted along the dreels, like the tents of concealed commanders. And indeed the hidden men are making quick decisions. They are grading the potatoes and placing them either in a bag at the end of the machine or in the large containers hauled along by another tractor.

ARDROSS FARM, OCTOBER 1988.

WINTERING

The interior of this wintering cow shed looks far from inviting. Now that winter is over the premises will be cleaned and painted. Only when the cattle return from pasturing, however, will the quarters return to life: a rich mingling of breaths and bodies as the herd huddles together for warmth.

ELIE, MAY 1987.

HEADS AND TAILS

The men bend to the shape of an imaginary pantomime horse—but the posture and the struggle are no joke. The harsh weather means winter shelter for the sheep and the 'tups' are brought indoors for breeding purposes—that is if you can catch them and persuade them to leave the bitter snows.

DRUMCARRO FARM, DECEMBER 1989.

IF WINTER COMES

When cometh Jack Frost? the children ask.

He sows his white seeds in winter and an eerie stillness hovers like a cloak over the woods and grasses. You can fairly feel the freezing grains along the top stones of the dyke.

BALCARRES ESTATE, JANUARY 1989.

71

THE SEA

WHEN VAUGHAN WILLIAMS set the lovely poem 'Linden Lea' to music, he was thinking of the idyllic seclusion of the old English countryside and not of the Scottish fisherman toiling at the nets in the middle of the storm-swept North Sea. Nevertheless the sentiments expressed in this verse hold true both for Somerset cider-maker and Fife fisher.

For the fisherman has no master but the sea: a master that he may love, fear, long for, grow weary of—but never despise. Respect is the fisherman's watchword and password. Only a fool goes to sea with no respect in his heart. To the wise fisherman the sea is god.

The fishermen of several decades ago went to sea not, as the song has it, to make money faster, but because it was the occupation that history, tradition, parentage, place and time had ordained for them. Often they toiled all night and caught nothing, for fishing is an act of faith. Even when they did haul on full, flashing nets, they never grew rich. Hard work and poverty went together, forming the spine of the East Neuk.

The fishing once made the havens of the east coast of Fife throb with economic life; the herring was the pulsating heart of its communities and the Firth of Forth was in those days shark-finned with Fifies (sailing vessels) and smoky with steam-drifters.

What happened after that is a sad story. Overfishing, new technology and lack of governmental foresight and control turned the firth into a graveyard of waves. Fishermen had to sail much further afield to make their catches and for a time indeed they did make money. The pictures of Pittenweem today may look healthy enough but the political writing is once again on the water. Look closely at these photographs of the busy, hard-working fishermen of East Fife: you may never see their like again.

LIGHT UNTO LIGHT

Looking eastward across a choppy Anstruther harbour. The Hannah Harvie lighthouse on the west pier leads the eye to the now automized lighthouse on the May Island. The Hannah Harvie was named after the Cheltenham lady who gifted it in 1880 to commemorate the birth of the great preacher, Thomas Chalmers, whose Memorial Church dominates the Anster skyline. On the Isle of May a light has burned for centuries. Even so it has collected many wrecks in its time.

ANSTRUTHER, MARCH 1990.

NAUTICAL KNOWLEDGE

To everything there is a purpose . . .
The complication of lines and spars speaks eloquently of the skills of seamanship. The true
sailor must know the function and value of every inch and working part of his craft.
PITTENWEEM HARBOUR, AUGUST 1988.

76

REFLECTIONS

'Light is the principal person in the picture,' Monet used to say. How he would have loved
to paint this one! The photograph captures the deceptively idyllic calm of the fishing
townships in summer, for the firth they look out upon is often a web of storms.

PITTENWEEM, AUGUST 1988.

77

OUT OF THEIR ELEMENT

Stacked like this on shore, awaiting repair, it is difficult to picture the stranded tangle of nets operating effectively at sea. Cast into the waves, they will mirror the fluidity of the water, taking their catch with lethal grace.

PITTENWEEM, MARCH 1990.

NET MENDING

Dave Anderson is exhibiting a skill once practised on the shores of Galilee, when the disciples were fishermen. They would not have worked with cigarette and can, but they knew, as our Scottish fishermen do, the wretchedness of torn nets. The traditional mending needle flashing in Dave's cunning hand was made in either wood or bone. Nowadays plastic ones are common.

PITTENWEEM HARBOUR, JULY 1987.

PETER'S FISHERMEN

Change the costumes and the metalwork and this timeless scene could be happening in
Palestine in the time of Christ—old and young fishermen mending their nets in the sun.
Damage can range from minor rents to gaping holes or the loss of an entire fleet of nets.

PITTENWEEM HARBOUR, AUGUST 1987.

CONSTANT HOPE, CONSTANT TOIL

The old time forest of masts is replaced these days by a conglomeration of aerials. Still, at the start of the prawn run, it is a busy scene, the skipper barely pausing in his work to speak a word or two, while the mended nets are taken aboard and the engineers measure the deck space, contemplating extra shelter for the crew.

PITTENWEEM HARBOUR, AUGUST 1987.

FISHBOXES

The piers of the East Neuk were once stacked high with these. Washed up along the coast, they provided village boys with first rate material for the building of rafts or the lighting of fires. Alas, the plastic ones which are fast replacing them are of little use to the children of the area. Nor are they popular with the fishermen.

PITTENWEEM, SEPTEMBER 1989.

82

MORE TO FOLLOW

The Shore Street houses of Pittenweem encircle the old arena of the sea. In the harbour *Launch Out* has just unloaded her catch early on a summer's morning and Jim Wood, the skipper, slings a box on board, ready for the next trip. Meanwhile *Guide Us* waits to unload her boxes.

PITTENWEEM HARBOUR, 1988.

THE HEART OF THE MATTER

The heart of the modern ship is her engine. The *Guide Us* underwent heavy surgery
alongside Anstruther pier during a howling gale and driving rain. Once dismantled, the
old engine was manhandled to the forward hatch and then hoisted by crane to the pier.
The new engine was installed by the reverse procedure and the removed sections of deck
replaced. Heart transplant complete, the vessel throbbed with new life.

ANSTRUTHER HARBOUR, FEBRUARY 1988.

84

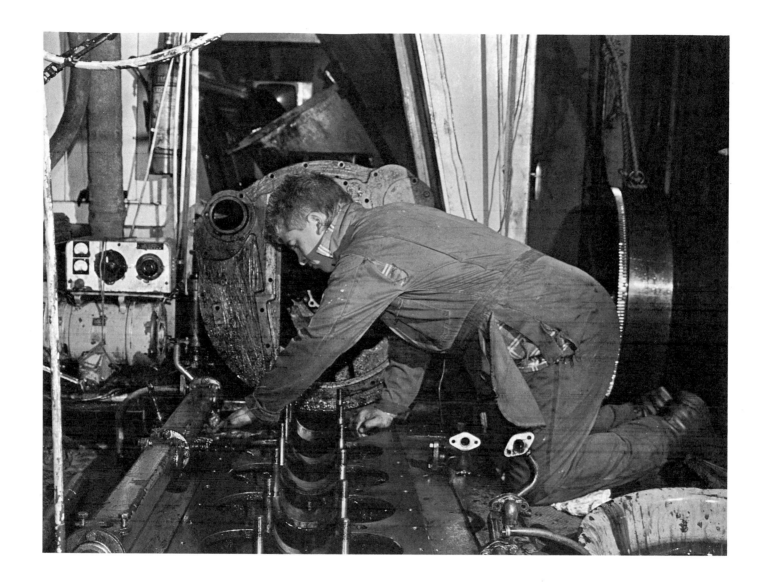

IN THE BOWELS OF THE SHIP

Once it was a matter of wood and canvas against wind and tide. Now the Fife fishermen
face different problems. The *Glen Alvah* was headed from Inverness to join the local boats
for the Pittenweem prawn run, when she ran her main bearings and had to be laid up for
repair. These lost days are the bugbear of the sophisticated engine age. In the time of sail or
steam even wild sea horses would not prevent some skippers from going to sea.

PITTENWEEM HARBOUR, MARCH 1988.

85

MUSCLE POWER

And the boat's muscles are its winch, which John Thompson has to check very carefully
before *Minnie Wood II* puts out to sea. A 'foul up' on this scale is no mere fankle but can
cost the boat dear.

PITTENWEEM HARBOUR, NOVEMBER 1988.

TALL AND TRIM

After her annual refit the *Minnie Wood II* stands proudly to attention, ready to receive her
Board of Trade Seaworthy Certificate and proceed to sea.

THE SLIP, ST MONANS, JUNE 1989.

THE ICE WAS ALL AROUND

The old boats went to sea packed with ice which the fishermen had broken up themselves.
Here at Pittenweem the ice is manufactured in the old granary, from which it is fed to the
various boats. On board *Launch Out*, Willie Donaldson and John Thomson direct the
spitting flow of ice below decks, where the fish will be stored in an arctic freshness.

PITTENWEEM HARBOUR, MARCH 1987.

88

EARLY TO WORK, EARLY TO RISE

For the men shown here the job begins earlier. It is Sunday afternoon and already the fleet
is putting to sea. When the world goes to work next morning the fisherman's week will be
well under way.

PITTENWEEM, SEPTEMBER 1988.

OUTWARD BOUND

Rolled to starboard, rolled to larboard

On to the fishing grounds with the boat heaving in the swell and the sea and sky about to change places.

THE NORTH SEA, MAY 1989.

FOR THOSE IN PERIL
The eyes and ears of the Maritime Rescue Service, the coastguard alerts and activates
where human lives stand the hazard of the sea.
CRAIL COASTGUARD STATION, MARCH 1988.

EARLY ONE MORNING

The hands of the old salts hauled unaided on hundreds of miles of sodden hemp. Nowadays even the old winch has been replaced with a 'block winch' which reduces the labour. Even so, bringing in the nets is backbreaking work, and as we witness here the last stages of the trawl, the morning sun has not yet cleared the skyline. Dawn and the fisherman are old friends.

5.30 HOURS, NORTH SEA, MAY 1989.

DAHN BUOY

The quiet skills of the fishermen, bringing on board the dahn buoy, are plied intently as the sea lurks insidiously just several feet away.

NORTH SEA, JUNE 1989.

HAULING

A young pair of hands learning an old skill: sorting out the net mouth as it comes on board
so that it will not fankle when it is shot again.

LAUNCH OUT IN THE NORTH SEA, MAY 1989.

FRUITS DE LA MER

Like a bulging basket of fruit, the net aboard *Launch Out* is about to be opened by Willie
Donaldson, and out will come spilling the sea's silver bounty—hundreds of flatfish
slipping aside to reveal the haddock, sole and cod at the centre of the net.

NORTH SEA, MARCH 1988.

95

NIGHT PILOTS

Attracted by lights and fish, the seagulls fly alongside like attendant spirits, eerily piloting the vessel home. Meanwhile the crew work all through the night, grading the catch, gutting and boxing—or throwing it back as too small, to the delight of the hovering beaks.

23.00 HOURS, NORTH SEA, MAY 1989.

FISH CLEANING

The fishermen's work is not confined to hauling and sweating. Most fishermen are also practised housewives! Adept at cleaning a fish, they can also prepare it for table and cook you a gourmet's delight once they reach home.

NORTH SEA, MAY 1989.

CROSSING THE BAR

Having faced the perils of the open sea, the East Neuk boats paradoxically come closest to danger at the very entrance to their home ports, which are treacherously narrow. The intrepid skipper must choose his moment, line the boat up, open his engine to full speed and make a run for the safety of the harbour. Here the *Launch Out*, skippered by Jim Wood, keels to port at 40 degrees, watching for the right moment in the teeth of the gale. The gulls accompany the last lap.

ENTRANCE TO PITTENWEEM HARBOUR, JANUARY 1989.

A WING AND A PRAYER

The sea boils white about the skerries as *Guide Us* comes safely to the halfway mark of the foaming harbour mouth. Skipper Willie Miller is not home yet, however, and the narrow neck of the entrance allows him no margin of error.

ENTRANCE TO PITTENWEEM HARBOUR, JANUARY 1989.

THE NIGHT OF THE HUNTER

In the dead watches of the December night the catches are landed. At 2 am the douce
Pittenweemers are fast asleep. The crews will join them for a few hard-earned hours
before setting off again for the winter fishing grounds, to hunt the cold soundless legions.

PITTENWEEM HARBOUR, DECEMBER 1988.

ANOTHER BOX, ANOTHER DOLLAR

The box is not full but the smile is broad. A summer's day, a Friday, a pretty girl
passing—to the hard wrought fisherman, safe again on shore, laughter costs nothing.

PITTENWEEM HARBOUR, AUGUST 1988.

AN OLD HAND AND A WHITE HEAD

History gets written into the flesh and the fishing is entered on the logbook of the skin.
Old Ferg, the oldest employee of the Fishermen's Mutual, helps with the early morning
landing of a catch. His white hairs have bent over many a silver fish in their time.

PITTENWEEM HARBOUR, APRIL 1988.

THE SILVER DARLINGS?

Romance reaches rock bottom when at the fishmarket the two sides of the industry perch
on the bodies of the slain and talk business. Every silver darling has its price.

PITTENWEEM FISHMARKET, JANUARY 1987.

IF THE PRICE BE RIGHT

The battle for the fish is fought not just at sea but here in the economic arena of the
fishmarket, where the cut and thrust continues over the catch.

PITTENWEEM FISHMARKET, JANUARY 1987.

LONELY NIGHTS
The catches landed and the crews dispersed, the boats are left alone with their lights and their reflections.

PITTENWEEM HARBOUR, NOVEMBER 1987.

106

OUR JAMES
Late at night and in the bleak midwinter *Our James* came home and the crew repaired their
nets under the arc lights of the boat, like actors in a timeless drama.
PITTENWEEM HARBOUR, JANUARY 1987.

107

EYES ON THE WATER

From his old boat, *The Trusty*, to the newer and bigger *The Provider*, Jimmy Linton is still
pulling in the lobster pots: a lifetime aligned to the sea.

WEST BAY, ELIE, MAY 1987.

CREEL MAKER

The oldest of the Crail fishermen, Jim Smith, sits in his workshop all the year round, alone with his lobster pots and his fourscore years. Making the pots is a traditional skill, though it appears from this picture that Bill has adopted plastic piping in favour of the old supple woodstems that took so long to gather and prepare and bend into hoops.

CRAIL HARBOUR, FEBRUARY 1986.

REMEMBRANCE

Sometimes I sits and thinks . . .

The old timer sits on the bollard but his thoughts follow the boat to sea long after it has disappeared. In his day he too was one of the men that go down to the waters to do business in great ships.

PITTENWEEM HARBOUR, 1986.

AFTERWORD

WITH A COURSE SET by experience, out they go, past the May Island
with its light flashing 'goodbye and good luck', out to the fishing grounds, where
the whales used to play and the fish danced in the net. To the sea of heaving decks
and sleet that cuts like a razor. To the lumps of water that can devour ships
leaving no trace, thoughts of these waves always on their minds but never
spoken.

The crew sheltering in the lee of the wheelhouse, trying to light a roll-up with
damp matches, thinking of home and warm dry bed. Then the skipper orders
them to start bringing the net inboard; soaked, and with hands like blocks of ice,
the muscles ache as they do his bidding. Soon the fish is graded, gutted, washed
and sent below for boxing with shovels of ice stowed ready for market. Just time
for that wonderful piping hot mug of sweet tea that is like fire in their throats,
before they shoot the nets again and again, each time they say 'please god let it be
full this time' . . .

Cliff Wilson